For Aaron and the Fly

British Library Cataloguing in Publication Data
Robinson, Colin
Bye-bye, fly!
1. Readers – 1950 –
I. Title
428.6   PE1119
ISBN 0-370-31108-6

Copyright © Colin Robinson 1987
Printed in Great Britain for
The Bodley Head Ltd
32 Bedford Square, London WC1B 3EL
by W. S. Cowell Ltd, Buttermarket, Ipswich
First published 1987

BYE-BYE, FLY!

COLIN ROBINSON

The Bodley Head
London

Mummy's home!

"What's for tea?"   Grandad heard something.

Scrounger sniffed something.

But Baby Jo saw the fly first.

"You won't catch it that way," said Mummy.

"No," said Baby Jo.

"I'll do it," said Mummy.

"No," said Baby Jo.

"I used to catch them with my bare hands," said Grandad.

"We'll *never* catch it this way."

"Where's tea? I'm hungry," said Mummy.

"Never mind, *I* know how to catch it," said Daddy. "Just watch me."

"Never mind," said Baby Jo.

"Bye-bye, fly."